P9-DWN-134

A Picture Book of
Harriet Tubman

by David A. Adler
illustrated by Samuel Byrd

Holiday House / New York

Text copyright © 1992 by David A. Adler
Illustrations copyright © 1992 by Samuel Byrd
Printed in the United States of America

Library of Congress Cataloging-in-Publication Data
Adler, David A.
A picture book of Harriet Tubman / by David A. Adler; illustrated
by Samuel Byrd.
p. cm.
Summary: Biography of the black woman who escaped from slavery to
become famous as a conductor on the Underground Railroad.
ISBN 0-8234-0926-0
1. Tubman, Harriet, 1820?–1913—Juvenile literature. 2. Slaves—
United States—Biography—Juvenile literature. 3. Afro-Americans—
Biography—Juvenile literature. 4. Underground railroad—Juvenile
literature. 5. Slavery—United States—Anti-slavery movements—
Juvenile literature. 6. Tubman, Harriet, 1820?–1913. [1. Afro
Americans—Biography. 2. Slaves. 3. Underground railroad.]
I. Byrd, Samuel, ill. II. Title.
91-19628
CIP
AC
ISBN 0-8234-1065-X (pbk.)

Other books in David A. Adler's *Picture Book Biography* series

A Picture Book of George Washington
A Picture Book of Abraham Lincoln
A Picture Book of Martin Luther King, Jr.
A Picture Book of Thomas Jefferson
A Picture Book of Benjamin Franklin
A Picture Book of Helen Keller
A Picture book of Eleanor Roosevelt
A Pictue Book of Christopher Columbus
A Picture Book of John F. Kennedy
A Picture book of Simón Bolívar

Harriet Tubman was born in 1820 or 1821 on a large plantation in Dorchester County, Maryland. Although the plantation had a big house with many rooms and fine furniture, Harriet was born in a small one-room log hut far behind the big house. The hut she was born in had a dirt floor, no windows, and no furniture.

Harriet was the sixth of eleven children. Her father, Benjamin Ross, and her mother, Harriet Green, were both slaves. They were owned by Edward Brodas. He owned Harriet Tubman, too.

The slaves worked hard all day, but they weren't paid.

Harriet hated slavery. She was wild and often beaten. She was not willing to do as she was told.

One time, when Harriet was "hired out" to work for someone else, she saw a bowl filled with lumps of sugar. She said later, "Now you know, I never had anything good, no sweet, no sugar, and that sugar right by me did look so nice." She took one lump from the bowl.

Harriet's mistress, Miss Susan, saw her take it and chased after her with a whip. Harriet ran from the house and hid with the pigs. She ate potato peelings and other scraps until she was so hungry she had to go back. When she did, she was whipped again and again.

Edward Brodas sold lumber, apples, wheat, and corn that grew on his plantation. Sometimes he took slaves he owned and sold them, too, "down the river" to plantations farther south. Harriet saw two of her sisters taken away in chains. Harriet was afraid that one day she would also be sold.

When Harriet was a young girl, abolitionists, people against slavery, were beginning to speak out and protest. Abolitionist newspapers were being published.

Nat Turner, a young slave, knew how Moses had led the Israelites from slavery in Egypt. He hoped to lead his people out of slavery, too, and in 1831 he started a rebellion. Slave owners, their wives, and their children were killed. Nat Turner and others were caught and hanged. Harriet dreamed that one day a true Moses would lead her to freedom.

In 1835, Harriet came between a master and a slave who was running away. The master threw a metal weight at the runaway. It hit Harriet instead and almost killed her.

Harriet had a deep cut in her forehead that never fully healed. For the next almost eighty years, Harriet suffered from severe headaches and sleeping spells. But she survived and thanked God for saving her. After the accident she often prayed.

In 1844, Harriet married John Tubman, a free man. They lived in his cabin near the Brodas plantation.

Harriet was thinking about running away. She wanted John to join her, but he wouldn't. He said that if she ran off he would tell her master and soon the patrollers and their dogs would be after her. But Harriet had made up her mind. She started planning her escape.

Slaves often sang in the fields. The afternoon before
Harriet ran off she sang, too, and in the words of her
song was a message to the other slaves.

"When that chariot comes,
I'm going to leave you.
I'm bound for the Promised Land."

For Harriet Tubman, the Promised Land was north,
where she would be free.

Harriet escaped at night with three of her brothers. They had no food, no money, and they didn't know where to go. Soon after they left, Harriet's brothers decided to turn back. They made Harriet go back, too.

Two nights later, Harriet went off alone. "I had a right to liberty or death," she said after her escape. "If I could not have one, I would have the other."

Harriet ran to the house of a white woman who had once offered to help her. The woman told Harriet which house to go to next. The people in the second house directed Harriet to another house farther north. Harriet was traveling on what was known as the *Underground Railroad*. Each stop on the *Railroad* was the house of someone who believed slavery was wrong and was willing to help runaway slaves find their way to freedom.

Harriet hid during the day. She traveled at night until she reached Pennsylvania. There was a law in that state against owning slaves.

Harriet Tubman was a free woman. She felt like a new person. She said later, "The sun came like gold through the trees and over the fields, and I felt like I was in heaven."

During the years between 1850 and 1860, Harriet worked as a cook, dish washer, and cleaning woman. She used much of the money she earned to make nineteen trips south to lead about three hundred slaves to freedom. Many of them were her own relatives.

MENU

RULES AND
REGULATIONS

Harriet took them from one safe house to the next. Sometimes she led them as far as Canada. She was a "conductor" on the Underground Railroad.

At times Harriet disguised herself as a weak old woman or as a man. She used songs as a secret code. When the runaways were hiding and it was safe to come out, she sang a joyful song, "Hail, oh hail ye happy spirits." The runaway slaves always recognized Harriet's deep, husky voice.

Once slaves began their journey north with Harriet, she wouldn't let them turn back. When slaves were too scared to go on, Harriet pointed a gun at their heads and said, "You'll go on, or you'll die."

Years later Harriet said proudly, "I never ran my train off the track. I never lost a passenger."

Harriet was called "Moses" because she led her people out of slavery. There was a huge reward waiting for anyone who caught her, but no one ever did.

In 1858 Harriet met John Brown, a leader in the movement to end slavery. He called her one of the best and bravest people in America. He called her "General Tubman."

In November 1860 Abraham Lincoln was elected president, and eleven southern states withdrew from the United States. They didn't want Lincoln, a man who hated slavery, as their leader.

The war between the north and south, the Civil War, began on April 12, 1861. During the war Harriet Tubman worked as a nurse and a spy for the northern army. She went into enemy territory and led hundreds of slaves to freedom. She helped care for slaves who ran north during the fighting.

In December 1865, soon after the Civil War ended, an amendment to the U.S. Constitution was passed. Slavery was no longer allowed in the United States.

After the war Harriet Tubman returned to her home in Auburn, New York. John Tubman had died in 1867. In 1869 Harriet married a former slave and soldier for the northern army, Nelson Davis.

In Auburn she went from house to house selling vegetables. Wherever she went she was asked to tell about her adventures on the Underground Railroad.

Harriet Tubman helped many former slaves who came to her in Auburn. She supported the suffragist movement, the fight for the right of women to vote in the United States.

Harriet helped establish a home in Auburn for sick, poor, and homeless black people. When she moved into that home in 1911, she was old and weak. "I can hear them bells a-ringing. I can hear the angels singing," she said. Soon after that, on March 10, 1913, she died. She was more than ninety years old.

Harriet Tubman was a brave, courageous woman. She was admired and loved by the many people who knew her. She was a conductor on the railway to freedom, a "Moses" to her people.

IMPORTANT DATES

1820 or 1821	Born in Dorchester County, Maryland. The exact date of her birth is unknown.
1835	Hit on the head with a metal weight while helping a slave escape.
1844	Married John Tubman, who died in 1867.
1849	Ran away from the Brodas plantation to Pennsylvania.
1850 – 1860	Led about three hundred runaway slaves to freedom along the Underground Railroad.
1862 – 1864	Worked in the Civil War as a nurse and spy for the northern army.
1865	The Thirteenth Amendment to the U.S. Constitution freeing all slaves in the United States was ratified on December 6.
1869	Married Nelson Davis, who died in 1888.
1908	Harriet Tubman Home for Aged and Indigent Negroes opened in Auburn, New York.
1913	Died on March 10 in Auburn, New York.